How Understanding the Priorities of Those Around Us Can Lead to Harmony and Improvement

By Landon T. Smith

Copyright 2017 by Landon T. Smith

Published by Make Profits Easy LLC

Profitsdaily123@aol.com

facebook.com/MakeProfitsEasy

Table of Contents

Introduction 4
Chapter 1: Understanding the Pyramid 6
Chapter 2: The Physical World 15
Chapter 3: The Safest are the Strongest 32
Chapter 4: Love and Connection 58
Chapter 5: Esteem Killers 80
Chapter 6: True Self-Esteem 90
Chapter 7: Are You Actualized? 105
Conclusion 112

Introduction

We all have needs! You have needs, I have needs, your neighbors have needs! But what exactly are those needs? Better yet, what even is a need? Many people go through this life with a great many needs, but so few of us truly understand what the nature of needs actually are. We have them, yes, but do we understand them? What's even the first step in being able to understand our needs?

Well, the good news is that we have a good friend of ours who had dedicated his life to understanding needs! His name was Maslow, and today we are going to be learning all about his valiant understanding of the human mind! Abraham Maslow was a psychologist who wrote a groundbreaking paper in the 40s talking all about the concept of needs. He invented a pyramid, known as the Hierarchy of Needs that would teach the world just how human beings related to the concept of needs.

The purpose of this book is to open your eyes and your mind not only to the concept of the hierarchy of needs, but also to the fact that it can aid you in your interaction with the world. If you've ever wondered how you can sufficiently motivate an employee, properly take care of your spouse, help your children live their lives to the fullest, then the Hierarchy of Needs is the tool for you!

Chapter 1: Understanding the Pyramid

Maslow's Hierarchy of needs is a large pyramid with several different sections to it. The entire purpose of designing the pyramid was so that Maslow could point to what would make for a self-actualized individual. Back in his time period, there was a great amount of emphasis on psychological malady. People were obsessed with neurosis, psychosis and the mental sickness of mankind. Extensive books on treatment were written and many people such as Freud and Jung had come onto the scene with bold claims on what it means to heal the mentally deranged and unwell.

Maslow, on the other hand, did not believe that psychology should only be restricted to that of the sick. Psychology to him was not just a study of the ill, but also of the exceptional. He focused his studies on those of humanity whom he considered to be exceptional people, such as

Einstein. He searched for evidence of what made humans exceptional. To him, it made little sense that we should only focus on the crippled, the sick and the weak. Rather, it would make for a far better case if we were to find a way to make humans better through studying the superior.

It was through this process that Maslow was able to come up with the Pyramid. The Hierarchy of Needs is essentially everything necessary in order to achieve self-actualization. What self-actualization means is that a person is able to recognize that they have potential and as such, pursue after that highest potential. A self-actualized individual is someone who believes in becoming the very best that they can and pursues it to all ends. This is what makes for a superior athlete, a genius or an entrepreneur. Rather than simply living a life of mediocrity, the self-actualized person seeks greatness for themselves.

Let's show a representation of the Pyramid of needs here.

5. Self-Actualization

4. Esteem

3. Love and Belonging

2. Safety

1. Physiological

Just like a pyramid, we begin from the bottom and work our way up in order of importance. The first thing that is the most important for a human being is the physiological needs such as food and water. Without those base physiological needs taken care of, a person will starve to death or die of dehydration, preventing them from becoming self-actualized at all.

Number two would be safety. In order for any individual or even a civilization to thrive and excel, they must be able to work freely and safely. Threat of danger, death or destruction can prevent a person from being able to make the most of their lives. This is why early man wasn't particularly innovative. A hunter with a spear and nothing else would be forced to travel from place to place, searching for a safe enough area for the time being. Until early man was able to sufficiently build safe places such as cities with big high walls, they weren't particularly innovative. Most real invention and transformation of our cultures began once we had the safety to think about other things.

The third on the list starts moving into the more emotional and relational areas. With the bottom two parts of the pyramid being about purely physical experiences, the third pillar is love and belonging. C.S Lewis once said, "Friendship is unnecessary, like philosophy, like art... It has no survival value; rather it is one of those things that give value to survival." Without love and belonging, there is very little reason for us to be alive, however it is not necessary for us to be able to survive.

The fourth moves even higher up in its reach and begins to focus less on external things, such as relationship or safety, and instead begins to focus on the actual individual themselves. Esteem means how a person relates to their own selves, how they look at their relationship with the world and most importantly, what they feel about themselves. Those who have great levels of self-esteem feel confident, strong and capable in their own skin. On the flipside, those who have low self-esteem tend to be sad, depressed or lonely. Esteem is necessary for a human to feel functional at their highest level.

The final piece to the pyramid is self-actualization. This is what happens after you have achieved significant mastery over the other four areas. This is where you are free enough to achieve incredible results and become a person who is fully alive, able to do great things without restriction.

As you can see, the Pyramid itself is a roadmap to success. Those who follow after it will end up living a great life! However, there are a lot of challenges in order to be able to make the very best of this pyramid. There is a challenge of learning how to dissect each area of the pyramid so that you can fully understand your own relationship with those needs. The good news is that is what our whole purpose is going to be with this book. We will take you through each need, chapter by chapter, and show you exactly what those needs are compose of, what the results of not having those needs fulfilled looks like and what you can do to evaluate your own needs.

Before we delve in deep, let's talk about what one of the biggest dangers behind reading these kinds of discussions is. The greatest danger when it comes to learning psychology and how human needs function is to neglect our own relationship with those needs. We can be tempted to read a book and think about how all the other people in our lives need this information so that they can change. In other words, if you are a manager or a spouse who is looking for a better way to motivate people, you might be tempted to look at this Pyramid as a to-do method so that you can help other people. This isn't ideal, primarily due to the fact that if you want to be able to help other people, you have to be willing to take a hard look at yourself first.

Think about how airplanes instruct parents in the event of an emergency. The first thing they tell all parents when the oxygen masks drop is to make sure that the parent focuses on putting their own oxygen mask on first. Now, a parent's first reaction is to ignore their own health and safety, and focus on getting the oxygen masks on their children. However, this is a problem! If the airplane loses pressure at a certain altitude, the people who are onboard have less than 20 seconds before they are knocked unconscious. The masks prevent a person from being knocked out or even killed by the change in air pressure. If a parent is struggling to put one oxygen mask on their first child and the air pressure changes, the parent will be knocked out and all of their children will be killed. However, if the parent is willing to put their oxygen mask on *first* and then take care of their children, everyone will be safe.

The temptation when it comes to looking at psychology and instruction manuals on how to inspire people is to ignore the fact that you as an individual need to have your oxygen mask on first. You must be willing and able to take all of the principles within this book and adopt them for your own, so that you are able to effectively and efficiently help others when the time is right. If you aren't looking to your own needs, if you aren't able to confirm that you are a healthy, self-actualized individual, those people whom you are trying to help will suffer and they will suffer immensely. The only way you can help others is to help yourself first.

This isn't the easiest pill to swallow, of course. Many of us like to believe that we are highly adjusted individuals, or that there is nothing wrong with us, but all I ask you is to keep an open mind as we begin to go through each part of the hierarchy and apply the principles and ideas to yourself first. You might learn a bit more about yourself than you realize and in the process, you will be able to grow as a person. Once you are able to have mastery over your own life, then you will be able to inspire others to grow and change, regardless of whether you are a manager, a church leader, a spouse or a parent.

Chapter 2: The Physical World

Humans are an interesting race. We are both physical and mental creatures. We have minds and bodies. In order for us to be entirely functional, we must be able to take care of both sections equally as well. Yet, no matter how healthy the mind is, no matter how functional or intelligent it is, without the body being taken care of, we will not be able to make full use of the mind. No matter what we do, if our bodies are not functional, we will have minimal impact on the world around us.

The concept of physiological needs can be broken down into several different sections: health, strength, hunger and sex. If each of these areas is met in some way, then a human will be able to function on higher levels. Let's look at each one and what it means for you.

Health:

Health is perhaps one of the most vital pieces to the physiological puzzle due to the fact that if we are not healthy, we will not be able to live well. Ask just about anyone out there who has a chronic disease or lives with some kind of disability, there is immense pleasure to be had in being healthy. Unfortunately, health is just something that most people end up taking for granted. This is a great tragedy, primarily because we only get one body. If we mess it up, that's it. There's no going back, there's no reversing the damage. Even as medical science increases in its ability to heal and cure diseases, there is no guarantee that they can reverse the damage that is done to our bodies.

However, most individuals tend not to pay any attention to their bodies. They consume terrible foods, take dangerous drugs and overindulge in chemicals that ultimately will wreck their health in the long run. When it comes to exercise and working out, they tend to ignore it in favor of just having fun. Ultimately, these kinds of lifestyles will lead to a life of sickness.

We need our health. We need it in order to survive. An individual who doesn't have their health will live a very unfortunate and frustrating life. There are things that we cannot avoid, such as genetic disorders, diseases we are born with and other factors that are outside of our control, but we do have the opportunity to have a great amount of control over those other factors. A self-actualized individual is someone who makes a consistent attempt to focus on taking charge of their health and striving to improve it.

So, what are some of the ways that we as individuals can take control of our health? Well, let's take a look at a basic list of things that you can do.

Health Actualization One: Knowledge

When was the last time that you had your immunizations taken care of? When was your last TDAP shot? What about your vitals? Your cholesterol, your blood sugar, etc. One of the most valuable tools that you can have when it comes to becoming an individual with an active interest in taking care of your health is knowledge. The more you know about your own body, your own statistics, the more sense of a direction that you will have.

It doesn't matter how old or young you are. You should have a general sense of what your vitals are at all times. They do fluctuate and change based off your actions and habits, so that means you must also be constantly renewing your information. This requires that you be willing to see a doctor every few months for checkups or physicals. While many people aren't fans of doctors or having their bodies examined, it is a necessary thing if you want to be secure in your physical needs.

A lot of times, our sicknesses are caused by unexamined needs. The body is a complex machine with a lot of things necessary to keep it functioning at all times. If you aren't sure what your body is needing, then it means that you aren't running it very well at all. The problem with the human body is that it can run at suboptimal levels and most people are used to that. They think that just because they can wake up in the morning and walk around, that means they are doing just fine. The truth is that unless you have an understanding of what your bodies needs in order to function well, you won't be running at your best. This requires you having a willingness to sit down and really study not just the human body but also your own so that you understand exactly how to care for yourself.

Health Actualization Two: Nutrition

Our bodies need fuel in order to move. We obtain that fuel through food. Oftentimes, food is looked at as simply a luxury or a pleasure. We enjoy eating and the human race has spent a tremendous amount of effort in creating culinary masterpieces. The problem is that in our modern lifestyle, we have often forgotten that food at one point was solely seen as a means to an end. Now with our fancy kitchens, greasy pizzas and succulent sweets, we treat food as the end. We rush to food and enjoy it greatly, and some end up entirely neglecting the nutritional aspects of it.

Food is great, there is no denying that. However, when we neglect our bodies nutritional needs, we are actually condemning ourselves to living a less efficient life. It can be easy to forget that we have nutritional needs past sating our hunger. When we are hungry, we can eat just about anything and feel full from it. However, just because you ate a big meal doesn't mean that you are getting the vitamins and minerals that your body needs. Someone who is self-actualized within the realm of health would pay attention to the amount of vitamins that are necessary in order to function *well*. The word well is key here, because the body can function with junk in it. It just won't function nearly as properly as a body that is being fueled by the right kinds of foods.

The better we fuel our bodies, the healthier we will become. And the less that we have to focus on our health, the more we can focus on the higher levels of the pyramid, it's as simple as that.

Health Actualization Three: Prevention

As the old adage goes, an ounce of prevention is worth a pound of cure. There is something important to be said in learning how to have a preventative mindset when it comes to your health. This kind of mindset requires a willingness to focus on taking action right now in order to prevent an illness from hitting you later. This would include:

- Regularly getting healthcare screenings for various illnesses and diseases
- Getting properly vaccinated and immunized during sickness seasons
- Exercising regularly so that your body's health is in top condition
- Consuming supplements and vitamins that contribute to the body's ability to fight sickness
- Avoiding areas that are breeding grounds for sickness
- Developing a firm hygiene routine that keeps you clean and free of bacteria

The next physiological need goes hand in hand with health: strength. When we use the word strength we are not referring to the ability to pick up heavy objects, but rather we are talking about your body's ability to endure hardship and strain in the physical world. Someone who is physically strong isn't just muscular or able to lift 300 pounds above their head, but rather they are able to be perfectly functional in this world. Let's look at the various areas of strength that a self-actualized person would focus on developing.

Strength Actualization One: Cardiovascular Health

Walking up three flights of stairs should not put someone in a state of severe breathlessness and exhaustion. Our cardiovascular health is a great indicator of our actual strength in the world. If your body is not able to endure some basic fitness things such as running, moving quickly, even walking at a fast pace, then you will not be able to have a great impact on the world. Not to mention, you are also physically vulnerable to danger at all times when you don't have a good cardio system. Imagine if there was some sort of danger or catastrophe that required you to move quickly, would you be able to survive?

On a physical level, our ability to function in the world around us requires us to have a decently developed cardiovascular system. However, in order for us to be able to excel, we must be able to increase our capacity for cardio work. Every human being, in order to truly be the most efficient, must be able to run a mile without stopping, swim a mile, climb up a rope and run up stairs, all without their heart giving out. This might seem like a silly task and it might even seem like it doesn't belong in a book about psychology, but the reality is that when you have the physical capacity to overcome physical obstacles, you are freeing up your mind to worry about other things.

When you are not in a place of cardiovascular fitness, there are things that can worry you. Long walks, hikes, fun runs or even things such as helping a person move, all of these can create a great degree of stress if you are not in the right kind of running shape. By having a confidence in your physical body at all times, you will reduce your stress level and increase your actualization!

Strength Actualization Two: Power

Not only must a person be cardiovascular fit in order to be self-actualized, they also need to have a great amount of power. This would be what we would consider to be the classical strength, based around the idea of lifting things, hoisting boxes and moving things aside. In our regular world, the idea of physical power has been reduced to little more than an amusement. Those who are strong tend to be people who lift weights for a hobby. Very few people focus on the functional aspect of strength training.

Just as with cardio, having a strong body allows for you to endure in times of great stress and tragedy. A self-actualized individual must never fall prey to the idea that they are immune to circumstances that require great strength. At any moment, the worst can happen, and your confidence in your ability to respond will be the difference between life and death. Don't just increase your lung capacity and your heart health, increase your muscular strength. It is of the utmost importance.

After strength comes the focus on hunger. Of course, hunger and thirst are simply binary situations. You are either hungry or you are sated. You are either thirsty or you are quenched. There isn't much to be done about either of those states other than take care of them. Although since we are on the subject of health and physiological strength, the average American is relatively dehydrated in their life. If you want to have a greater level of self-care in your life, then you might want to consider making sure that you are drinking sufficient amounts of water each and every day.

After hunger comes the final physiological need: sex. Sex is a very complex need as it is something that is biologically driven in just about every human. While it is true that there are people in this world who are asexual, meaning they don't have a sex drive, most people would have some level of sex drive that exists.

Sex drive on a biological level comes from the basic human instinct to procreate. Humans feel an intense urge for sex based on their body's biological rhythms. There are many things that can increase or lower a person's sex drive, such as hormones or physiological factors, but ultimately the purpose of the sex *urge* itself is an evolutionary trait adapted so that people would be able to populate the earth.

On a needs level, sex is nothing more than an expression of a primal need to replicate. While that doesn't sound particularly romantic, it is true. We feel a pressure to have sex because it is our body's way of furthering the species. Our intellectual selves, the higher self, creates the concept of sex being for pleasure, romance and intimacy but the reality is that we are sexual creatures purely because of our biological demands. If those biological pressures were switched off, people would be a lot less apt to have sex.

What makes sex one of the more interesting physiological needs is the fact that the need comes from a global purpose: furthering the human race. As stated before, that is why we feel that pressure. However, it is also the only need that we have that can go unfulfilled without it killing us. We need air, water, food and our health, but even though sex is a basic human need, we can live without it. What does this mean on a self-actualized level? Well, for starters it means that if we can understand why we have that need, we can put it in the proper place.

One problem that many cultures falls into is the fact that sexual desire can easily outpace common sense. A man who is searching for sexual release can get himself into a lot of trouble by attempting to impress the opposite sex with acts of daring and cunning. In the moment, the man might believe that he is expressing his desire for romance, but when a physical need pushes you so hard that you act in a manner that could adversely affect you, it's not romance but basic biology. We are more than biological creatures, of course, and we have the ability and option to resist our own sexual urges. There is nothing wrong with consistent, steady expression of sexual function, however, we must be aware that a great many times we can be led into poor decisions due to our sexual desires.

Think about the individual who is engaged in a relationship that is quite detrimental to their health. They might be with an abusive partner, or frankly a partner who is highly erratic and could be defined as crazy. Yet despite how clear it is to just about everyone around that individual, the person in question remains oblivious to the danger of the relationship. Why is that? Primarily because the sex drive's job isn't to evaluate whether a mate is suitable or not, honestly the sex drive's job is to create another human. Since we have the power to control our reproduction through use of condoms or other means of birth control, we can enjoy all of the benefits of sex without that procreation.

The solution to the problem of having a strong sexual desire override your common sense is to take a step back and recognize that sexual desire is nothing more than a hunger. And unlike our regular hunger, there are no long-term consequences to going without sex (no matter what our society says.) There is a proper place for sex in the human life, but the self-actualized individual is one who is able to keep it in the right box for the right time. More importantly, they're the kind of person who are able to resist giving into their human urges that would lead to detrimental results.

Ultimately, if we are able to take care of our physiological needs on a regular basis, we should be able to function at a much higher level. Believe it or not, but a great many people in this world end up neglecting their own physiological necessities for a host of reasons. Take some time to examine your own life and ask yourself, are you taking care of your needs? Are you handling your health properly? Are you making sure that you are able to sufficiently interact with your world? If you find that there are some areas that are lacking, that's a good thing! The first step on the road to self-actualization is what Maslow referred to as metacognition. Metacognition is essentially the idea of knowing about knowledge. In other words, it means that since you know there is something missing in your life, you have the ability to work on it. You have the capacity to see a shortcoming and fix it, because of your metacognition!

Once you've accurately assessed where you are with your health, it's time to move onto the next level of the pyramid: safety.

Chapter 3: The Safest are the Strongest

Have you ever felt unsafe before? Maybe you were in a bad part of town and saw someone sketchy following you. Perhaps you heard a loud crash in the middle of the night, right outside your house. Maybe a car on the highway is weaving in and out of traffic, causing you to worry about an imminent crash. Either way, when you are in a moment of feeling unsafe there is honestly only one thing that you can think about: the danger.

Under the Hierarchy of Needs, we find that safety is one of the most vital parts of reaching self-actualization. As the second-tier need, we find that without safety, we cannot truly move up into the higher levels of thought. Yet, while we live in a world where there are relatively higher amounts of physical safety, there are more than one types of safety to consider. There are essentially three different types of safety: Physical safety, emotional safety and financial safety.

Safety more or less dictates a society's ability to get things done. If they are always focused on defending themselves from barbarian attacks, they don't have the free time to think about thinks like art, philosophy or science. This is equally true on an individual level. If we are unable to protect ourselves from danger, be it emotional, physical or financial, we will always be consumed with our attention towards whatever the danger is. Just ask a person who is teetering on the edge of bankruptcy how productive they are in their free time, they'll tell you they aren't!

If you want to reach the higher echelons of the pyramid, then you must be willing to secure your own life in those three areas. This is not an easy thing to do at all. Most people have the first area, physical security, locked down pretty well. They live in a first world country where there is very little immediate danger, but when it comes to the second and third types, you'll find that a great many people in this world aren't sufficiently providing for themselves. Let's break down each category piece by piece and see what achieving safety in each area entails.

Physical Security:

Being physically safe is one of the most important things you can work towards in your life. If you aren't physically safe, then it means that your life is in some sort of peril. It detracts from your quality of life, your ability to think, increases your stress level and puts you at a great degree of risk. Therefore, it is in your best interest to be an individual who focuses on making sure that your physical security is taken care of.

There are basics of physical security, such as shelter, that are pretty much a given in this culture. We won't go into those specifics due to the obvious nature of obtaining a home or place to stay. However, there are some areas of physical security that haven't been touched upon as greatly in our current society. Let's take a look.

Security Actualization One: Combat Competency

One of the disadvantages in living in a society where we have, for the most part, gotten past a constant occurrence of violence is the fact that since we no longer expect violence, we are no longer prepared for it. This is problematic when it comes to becoming safe and secure, because a great part of being safe is having the capacity to keep yourself safe. Since security has been relegated to a public service, such as the police, we have seen a diminished sense of responsibility for one's own safety.

A self-actualized individual is one who is able to sufficiently work for their own betterment and does not rely on externals to empower them to achieve things. This also applies when it comes to learning how to protect yourself. If you leave your own self-protection into the hands of other people, you are essentially abdicating your own responsibility in the matter. At the end of the day, no one is going to protect you better than yourself. This is counter-intuitive to the general thought of the population, who generally believes that the police are the best bet for our safety and survival.

The problem, however, is that the police are not always there to protect you. Others aren't always there to help you out. In fact, in most court rulings, it has been proven that the police do not have a duty to protect. This means that even though a cop will try and protect you if they can, they have no moral obligation under the court of law. Therefore, it is up to you to be able to protect yourself.

The easiest way to learn how to protect yourself is to obtain some level of combat training. This would mean either taking some self-defense courses, finding a personal trainer who can teach you how to fight or just taking up a combat hobby, such as boxing. If you want to be fully capable as an individual, then you must be willing to spend the time necessary to learn how to protect yourself. Don't fall for the false idea that other people will be able to save you. In the end, you are responsible for your own safety.

Security Actualization Two: Insurance

Another neglected piece of security is making sure that you are properly secured in the case of an emergency. Proper planning ahead is necessary if you want to be successfully free from the worry and obligation that keeps us operating out of the lower levels exclusively. The more concerned we become about our own security, the less we're able to focus on the more important things in our life. One concern that often crops up is the concern of handling disasters and emergency.

The world we live in is a risky one. One of the most powerful ways to mitigate risk in your life is by purchasing insurances of different types. There's health insurance, fire insurance, car insurance, etc. All of these things are designed to reduce the amount of risk that we have in our lives. By paying for insurance now, we are able to insulate ourselves from disaster in the future. Yet, there are people who are insurance averse for a number of reasons. The biggest reason is that the cost of insurance can give the appearance that it is a waste of money. Yet the problem is that insurance is only necessary when some disaster happens. We have no way of predicting our health, our physical safety or the safety of our property, meaning that it is all about risk management. The question isn't about whether or not insurance is a waste of money, but rather whether it is worth investing your money into protection from risk.

A self-actualized individual is one who is able to be free from the bondage that disaster brings. When your home is destroyed, when your car gets stolen or if you incur a serious medical problem, it will bring about a lot of stress, financial burden and pain. There are things that we cannot insulate from, such as the stress and emotional suffering that comes along with disaster, but there are things that we absolutely have the power to protect ourselves from. By making sure that you have the right kind of insurance policies and that you are covered, you can protect yourself from the immense financial burden that can be placed upon you when you get sick, get in an accident or lose your home.

While this discussion might seem somewhat out of place when it comes to learning self-actualization, you must realize that a self-actualized individual is free above all else. Financial burdens caused by disasters can drag us down into survival mode and distract us from being able to engage in higher thinking. It is very hard to have a free kind of mindset when you are completely overwhelmed with your financial health and future. Likewise, if you aren't able to pay for a necessary medical procedure, your health will threaten your ability to reach those higher levels. Ultimately, it is necessary for you to do everything that is possible to reduce risk in your life. There is no getting around it. Disaster is certain to come, no one is exempt from this. However, you have the ability to prepare for disaster adequately and shield yourself from the brunt of it.

Financial Security:

We live in a world that is more or less run by money. Everything costs money and you can't really survive in this life without having some kind of financial situation. Without money, you can't afford food, a house, a vehicle or medicine for when you get sick. Most of us make enough to get by, but more and more we are seeing households that are living paycheck to paycheck. This is problematic for those of us who want to reach the higher stages of self-actualization primarily because when we are living on a shoestring budget, we are half a step away from financial disaster. We must be secure, not only in the fact that we have a roof over our heads, but also in the fact that we are financially safe.

Financial security allows for us to function with significantly less stress in our lives. Finances have been cited as one of the most common things married couples fight about. While many people like to say "money doesn't bring happiness," they are often painting an incomplete picture of what money provides. Money isn't just about bringing us happiness by buying us jet skis, gold necklaces and things that no one needs, but rather money can provide us with lives of comfort and safety. Money doesn't buy happiness, but it does provide stability. We tend to function on a healthier level when we aren't constantly worrying about where our next paycheck is coming from or how we're going to make rent this month. Ask anyone who's had to scramble to pay all of their bills on time. It is a stressful, exhausting and emotional affair. It is extremely distracting and when you're busy focusing on how to buy food or pay rent, you aren't able to focus on improving yourself as a person.

If you are serious about being in total control of yourself, then there are financial actions that you must take in order to ensure your security. Let's look at them.

Financial Self-Actualization One: Independence

The word self-actualized means that you are able to achieve actions on your own, pushed forward by your own drive. There is a strong need for independence in the self-actualized individual. However, if we are financially dependent, we lose our sense of control over our own destinies. We are no longer capable of getting our own goals met and realized, instead we are beholden to another party. Dependence for financial security can crush our ability to achieve greatness. Instead of being concerned with the things that make us happy, we are forced to become concerned with the things that make other people happy.

There are many different ways a person can be leashed into financial dependence. For example, a young adult who is financially dependent on her parents will be forced to take the college major of their choosing. She might want to go into art or philosophy, but they will demand she goes into law. Since the young woman has no financial independence, she is unable to be fully free.

Another example is when a person who is deeply in debt considers changing jobs. They might be miserable where they work, but the debt prevents them from taking a risk in finding a new line of work. They aren't truly independent because they are forced to make decisions based on paying back their debt.

Sometimes we have obligations that we can't really get around, such as financial obligations to taking care of a child or paying for your mortgage, but those things don't restrict your independence because you chose to take on those roles. You are free in the sense that you decided that you wanted a home or a child. However, there are a great many financial situations that can take away that sense of freedom.

The greatest solution to being financially dependent, either on a specific job, a person or due to a debt is to work towards the goal of being financially independent. This is no small task, however. It will require focus, discipline and a comprehensive understanding of financial literacy. However, the good news is that it is possible. Most people have the ability to become self-actualized within their finances, if only they would choose so.

The major detractor from a financially independent lifestyle is the fact that it is a painful road. Saving doesn't feel very good in the moment, but over the long term, you will find that savings is one of the most important things that you can achieve in your life. There really is no replacement for financial independence. Nothing will be better than knowing that you are safe from having to worry about a job loss. You will experience a distinct pleasure once you realize that no one can control you because they have money and you don't. It is worth the hard work and sacrifice to find that independence.

Financial Self-Actualization Two: Education

Going hand in hand with independence is education. The greatest danger to our financial security is ignorance. If you don't have a comprehensive understanding of how money, the stock market, variable interest rates, credit scores and mortgages work, you can be certain that you are at a real disadvantage. Financial literacy is one of the most important things that you can have when it comes to taking control of your own destiny, primarily because the more you know about money, the more you can make it work for you.

A great amount of people in this world have a very vague understanding of how financial institutions affect them. As a result, they are very vulnerable. If we are going to be safe and sound financially, we must be educated, it is simple as that. Fortunately, it isn't particularly hard to learn about financial information these days, as there is a great amount of information available about it online. You can easily take a class online, watch a Youtube series or just read a few books about it and be well educated past the average American.

Financial Self-Actualization Three: Emergency Fund

As discussed in the insurance section earlier, mitigating and reducing risk is one of the most important parts of being safe. In the financial sense, it goes far beyond just getting some insurance, rather it is about learning how to craft a lifestyle that supports you in dire emergencies. In other words, the best action you could possibly do is to have an emergency fund.

An emergency fund is essentially a special kind of savings account where the money is only touched in the case of an emergency. This is the kind of fund that is accessed when you have a car repair needed, there's some kind of serious damage to your home or you need quick money to pay for an unexpected bill. The emergency fund is essentially the financial version of a get out of jail free card. It is there for you whenever you need it the most.

An emergency fund should not be underestimated. It is one of the most important weapons that you can have in the quest for financial security. It will help prevent unexpected financial problems from putting you behind in your regular finances. Most importantly, when you have a large financial cushion that can prevent you from getting in trouble, it provides you with a sense of security and wellness.

Everyone has different needs when it comes to an emergency fund, but the best option would be to have enough money to cover at least three months' worth of your expenses. This means that if your total expenses are $2,000 a month, you should have $6,000 squirreled away into a bank where you can't touch it unless of an emergency. This might seem like a lot of money to save, but it is the key to being safe and sound. That kind of cash stored up will provide you with a great amount of peace of mind and that is worth a lot!

Emotional Security:

Once we are no longer worrying about the physical or financial dangers in our lives, we must then turn our attention to the emotional dangers that can be present. You might be tempted to not worry about the emotional state and just focus on only financial and physical security, but don't be fooled! Our emotions play a pivotal role in how we function on a daily basis. If we are feeling emotionally threatened or in a place where our emotions are being toyed with, we won't have the ability to function as well as we'd want. When you are overwhelmed by sadness, consumed by rage or struggling with depression, it is significantly harder to be productive.

A self-actualized individual must be able to take care of their emotional state and safeguard it from harm, so that they are able to be functional. People with poor sense of emotional regulation or who are constantly being bombarded with negative feelings tend to rarely have the ability to be self-actualized. Let's look at some areas to focus on as you develop a greater sense of emotional security.

Emotional Self-Actualization One: Toxicity

There is a certain class of people in this world who are very unhealthy to be around. They have negative attitudes, they are rude and worst of all, they cannot stand to have other people happy. These are the kinds of folks who are self-obsessed. They play mind games. They cut you down. The worst part is that just about everyone has a friend or two who is like that. This is troublesome for a variety of reasons, the biggest being that the more toxic your friends are, the more they are going to affect you.

It has been said that you are the summary of the five people that you spend the most time with. People radically change in temperament, personality and thought process based around the company that they keep. This makes the relationships that you have of the utmost importance. If you are surrounded by toxic people, they will have a profoundly adverse effect on your own emotional health and wellbeing.

Yet many of us end up trapped in relationships with people whom we don't really like, but we have no way of getting out. At least, that's what we tend to believe. We act as if we have no choices but to be in these bad relationships. Either we feel guilty for wanting to leave, we feel a sense of obligation that we have to be their friend or we are just simply too afraid of being honest enough to cut it off. Toxic people tend to be difficult to get rid of, usually because they have some method of endearing themselves to us. They might use the age of the relationship against us, saying things like "we've been friends for x years and we don't turn our back on each other!" They might use their own good behavior towards you as a way to keep you obligated. The problem with this is that relationships are not transactional. You do not rack up debts within a relationship at all. A friendship or a romantic relationship is built around mutual trust and respect. You do nice things for your friend because you like them, not because they helped you out.

Toxic people try to drag relationships into a transactional system because that is usually where they have the most amount of leverage. They might be a chatty, gossipy bully who likes to mock your clothing, but they also take you out for drinks and pick up the bill every few weeks. This creates a sense of you owing them something. Truthfully, this is a warped perception. You don't owe your friends anything. A friendship must be built around mutual trust, love and respect. You don't get those things out of obligation, in fact, if they were obligations, they wouldn't be about love or trust anymore. Rather, they would be about paying debts. How many people want their relationships to be like that?

Truthfully, if you are allowing negative people to drag you down, you must be willing to have the honesty and the responsibility to sever the relationship. It might be hard, but it is worth it in the long run. Don't let your life be dictated by people who will bring you down. Nothing in this life is worth the pain and hardship endured by having the wrong kind of people in your world. Cut the relationship and save your own life.

Emotional Self-Actualization Two: Emotional Regulation

Our emotions are tricky things. They can be overwhelming and frustrating if we aren't able to regulate them properly. One major problem in the modern-day world is that many of us aren't taught how to handle our emotions the right way. We are taught either to suppress them, pretend like we don't feel them or to just simply ignore them in favor of doing more work. This kind of attitude toward emotions is very unhealthy, because it leads to long-term emotional instability. The more you try to repress or not feel your own emotions, the worse off you are going to be in the long run.

If we are to become self-actualized individuals, then we must be willing to learn how to handle our own emotions properly. This can be difficult, but what is worse is when we are threatened by our own emotions constantly. A neurotic individual who suffers from constant mood swings will not be able to focus on the higher levels of human thought, they will be far too busy dealing with anxiety and sorrow.

There are many different ways to learn emotional regulation. It is not something that you will master immediately, rather it takes a lifetime to be able to truly learn how to regulate your own emotions. Please note that we use the word regulate instead of control. Many times, a person is told to control their emotions, but in reality, they are just being told to suppress them. Emotional regulation is about being able to process through the emotions that you are feeling without being overwhelmed by them. Suppression is not in the equation.

One surefire method to learn emotional regulation is to spend some time identifying your emotions. We often feel many different feelings during the intense parts of our day, but how many of us are able to identify them? By learning to slow down, take a deep breath and identify what you are feeling, it will give you a greater method of control.

There are many different resources available for emotional regulation. There are books, seminars, videos and even people who are willing to teach you how to learn to regulate your feelings. If you are someone who is constantly under barrage from your emotions and you aren't sure why, you might even want to consider going to a professional therapist. They are often very quick ways to learn how to get a handle on your own feelings.

Emotional Self-Actualization Three: Strong Relationships

We are relational creatures. There is no getting around the fact that we were designed to be in relational function with one another. In the first part of this section, we discussed the need to get rid of toxic relationships. That is a very good thing for your emotional freedom, however, it is not the only thing necessary for you to become emotionally self-actualized. You must also be willing to have strong relationships that build you up.

This is where many of us can struggle. It is easy enough to know that there are types of people to avoid in this world, but when it comes to finding good people, we just aren't sure what to look for. Many people end up thinking that it is better to go alone, frustrated that they can't find meaningful relationships. Some might not even try to find good friendships for fear that they will be rejected.

Ultimately, human beings need each other in order to excel. A good friend will make the difference in how you are able to achieve greatness in your life. Don't neglect the basic human need for relationships. In the next pyramid, we'll discuss this in detail, but for now, just take note that we need to have people in our lives in order for us to become emotionally secure.

So, those are the three types of securities that we need in order to be safe in today's modern world. We must be physically, financially and emotionally safe, so that we can function and excel properly. Yet, after we have a strong sense of safety, we can then go on to building up a community around us. Community isn't necessary for survival for the most part, but it is necessary for us to start moving up into the higher echelons of self-actualization.

Chapter 4: Love and Connection

With the third step of the pyramid, we begin to leave behind the concept of physical and physiological necessities and into mental and spiritual necessities. The third pyramid square is known as Love and Belonging. The need to belong and the human desire to love is one of the most powerful drives within humans. However, when there is a lack of love or belonging in a person's life, they will often begin to experience a significant amount of sorrow and sadness. Many people can even lose the will to live when they are unable to experience a true sense of belonging.

We would classify the need for love and belonging into three distinct areas: intimacy, friendship and community. Each one of these areas will actively help (or harm) a person's spiritual and emotional development, if they are properly experienced. If there is a deficiency in one or more of these areas, a person can begin to experience a variety of side effects. Let's go ahead and cover each area in detail.

Intimacy:

The word intimacy has often been associated with sexual contact. In our modern culture, if you were to say that a man was intimate with his wife, he would be having sex with her. However, the word for intimacy doesn't necessarily mean having sexual relations. In fact, the word intimacy essentially means closeness. Of course, in a sexual relationship there is a certain degree of closeness between the partners, but sexual intimacy is only a type of intimacy. There are, in fact, four different types of intimacies that exist.

- **Physical**: The physical intimacy where physical contact is occurring, creating a bond between the people. This could be seen as holding hands, kissing, hugging, draping an arm around someone. On a physiological level, whenever we have positive physical contact with *anyone* it actually releases oxytocin, a chemical that reduces stress and pain. That's right, there are physical benefits to physical intimacy that go beyond sex. This is why fathers of newborn babies are encouraged to hold their child skin to skin, because it creates a powerful release of oxytocin, which bonds the two together. The mother, of course, experiences a massive flood of oxytocin during childbirth, which immediately bonds her to the child. Therefore, if we are looking to have a higher degree of intimacy with someone, even in a non-sexual manner, it would be more beneficial if were to actually touch them on a regular basis. This only works when the physical affection is reciprocated, of course, if the person isn't interested in being touched, then it won't help at all.

- **Emotional:** Emotional intimacy is all about how a person makes you feel. When words are shared, when ideas and thoughts are crossed over from one person to another, it can bond us on an emotional level. Once a person feels safe with another person, they will naturally begin to bond. Their emotional vulnerability will increase and they will begin to experience a greater degree of personal connection. This is also where romantic relationships form as well, if there is any degree of attraction between the individuals.
- **Intellectual:** Intellectual intimacy is the experience of having someone else on your own intellectual level. A lot of times, we would use the word colleague to indicate someone whom you have intellectual intimacy with.

This is the person that you can enjoy a spirited debate with, or have a deep philosophical discussion. The more that you communicate with an individual on an intellectual level and the more they reciprocate, the greater this increases your intimacy with them.

- **Experiential:** Experiential intimacy is when you are engaging in the same activity as someone. It doesn't necessarily mean that you are talking or discussing things, but rather you are engaging in a mutual activity. For example, someone who is playing a sport with his friends is developing a form of experiential intimacy because they are doing something together and building a bond.

Ultimately, we need intimacy in our lives if we are going to be able to function well. The reason is that intimacy creates a sense of belonging and a feeling of closeness. Without those feelings of closeness, we tend to grow distant or even depressed. The cool thing about intimacy is that of the four listed, you don't need to have all of them to feel fulfilled. A person who isn't able to have physical intimacy due to lack of romantic relationships is still able to experience intellectual or emotional intimacy with their friends.

It is unfortunate, but in our current cultural climate, there is a great deal of awkwardness behind non-romantic types of intimacy. Many bids for closeness in our culture can often be mistaken for or labeled as sexual, even if it is not. A great deal of humanity craves connection, and sexual intimacy is only a specific type. However, most people these days do not find robust, close relationships due to the fact that they do not want to be considered to be weird or creepy. This can be scene mostly in male relationships.

There was a time when male relationships were normal and natural, however, with the rise of homosexuality in the world, it has created a tension between straight men who want to be close and intimate with each other, without any kind of sexual action. This isn't to blame homosexuality, of course, but rather to point the finger at society which has created the concept that deep, close relationships must always be of a romantic or sexual nature. Even when we see men engaging in intimate, non-sexual relationships, our culture will mock and tease them, calling it a bromance. This actively discourages men from seeking out close relationships for those fears.

Female relationships tend not to have this level of strain, as they have been traditionally considered to be the more emotional of the male/female dichotomy. This, of course, is a myth and continues to harm both genders. It harms men because it convinces them that they aren't meant to enjoy deeper relationships, and must keep their feelings and emotions bottled up. Having a close friend provides us with the space to be able to effectively vent about our feelings.

It doesn't matter what gender you are, you need intimacy in your life. And there isn't just romantic intimacy that you can engage in. It might seem weird or uncomfortable, especially considering out 21st century virtues, but the reality is that without intimacy, we as a species are not able to live to our full potential. The space and safety that deep, close relationships give us is irreplaceable. If you aren't searching for these relationships and you don't have any intimacy with people, then you must make it a point to start looking. You won't be able to reach the higher levels of self-actualization without it!

Friendship:

Friendship is similar to intimacy, although it is less intense and more widespread.

You can have a great many friends without having to have intimacy with them. There are different degrees of friendships in this life and all of them have different types of benefits. A well-rounded individual is someone who is able to have a good amount of all of those types.

Hobby Friendships:

A hobby friendship is a relationship that is built around a hobby of some sort. It is usually something like watching sports, playing video games together, even watching movies. We need surface relationships in our lives because it gives us a great amount of pleasure to engage in a mutual activity with a friend. We need people in our lives where we can just unwind with them. No matter what the subject is, there are times when a person just needs to get away from their anxieties and fears. A friendship based around a hobby will provide you with a necessary outlet to get away from the hardships of life.

Work Friendships:

A much-neglected area of the modern American life, the work friendship is one that is based around proximity due to working for the same company. The workplace can be a place of competition, backbiting, politics and disagreement, contributing to a great amount of stress and frustration in just about everyone involved. But the workplace doesn't need to be like this in every aspect. Rather, we as people need friends that we can work alongside with just as much as we need hobby friendships. Having a good workplace friend can make the job so much more bearable and enjoyable. The problem is that many people view the workplace as a primary place of competition. Most folks want to move up in the world and in order to do so, they are willing to step on each other and stab others in the back.

This hypercompetitive mindset isn't particularly healthy for a functioning friendship, however. If you do want to have a few good workplace friends, then you must be willing to let go of your ambition and stop looking at people as rungs on a ladder to climb. If you don't have that negative attitude, great! However, you still need to be careful that you aren't befriending people who have that perspective. Becoming good friends with a shark isn't the best idea, because they will most probably use you in order to get higher up on the ladder.

Now, office relationships come easy. People don't really have a choice to have a relationship with you when they work with you and see you every day. However, office friendships require more work. Just because you can all joke, laugh and tell stories doesn't mean that you are in a friendship. A workplace friendship must exist outside of work on some level. This requires effort and energy on your part. You must be willing to try and take your workplace relationships to a deeper level. Having a quick chat during lunch breaks doesn't make for a friendship, nor does palling around during a company outing. What makes for a good friendship is when you are willing to take time out of your own life to spend with them. Work is mandatory, friendship is not. By showing them that you are willing to build a relationship outside of the office, it will increase the strength of the relationship inside the office. Then you know you have someone that you can count on, someone that you can trust. That is definitely worth the work required!

Physical Friendship:

We all need close friends, even if it is just one person. It is unfortunate, but with the rise of social media and things such as Facebook, there has been an increased amount of people not experiencing close friendship. The computer screen has the ability to simulate a relationship, it can allow you to join a conversation between friends at a moment's notice. It lets you see all about a person's life, you can hear their stories and watch them talk about things live. All of these electronic means of relationship building can create the illusion of depth, but the problem is that online relationships or relationships through things like Facebook or Twitter suffer from a surprising lack of connection. They give the illusion that you are able to connect to people, but in reality, we were not designed to interact via a screen.

Studies have shown that those who engage in relationships through social media networks tend to experience greater feelings of depression, isolation and even envy. The reason we feel this way is primarily because social media gives a person the ability to filter what you see. This is amplified past the regular way that we communicate with people in the physical world. For example, your friend, who's really dealing with financial hardship and relational strife, can create a powerful picture of how amazing their life is by carefully editing their Facebook feed and showing dozens of pictures of them traveling, having fun and living life to the fullest. You don't see any of the dark corners of their life, you don't see any of the emotionally draining situations that they are in. Instead, you see a picture perfect, Truman Show-esque version of their lives where everything is carefully maneuvered to make you think their lives are prefect.

This picture-perfect life that is presented can create a feeling that we are somehow less interesting than our friends. It creates a powerful fear of missing out and a belief that our lives aren't nearly as interesting or wonderful as our friends. This creates a tension between us and our relationships with other people, creating jealousy and strife. It ultimately divides us and creates a sense of utter loneliness.

The solution to the dangers presented to us by social media is to learn how to develop real relationships in the physical world instead of assuming that we can have satisfying online relationships. There is nothing wrong with having online only friends, but it will never replace the standard face to face human interaction that we were designed to experience. Getting to meet a person in the flesh allows for true connection, whereas connecting to people online is a deeply isolating experience, regardless of whether you have a good time or not. There is nothing in this world that can replace regular human contact, no matter how hard you might try.

Best Friends:

A best friend can be hard to come by in this world, but they are definitely worth it. They are the kind of person that we can share our lives with, depend on in the worst of situations and generally seek wisdom and counsel from. Yet many people in America don't have a best friend. In fact, 92% of men report that they don't have a best friend. It can be really hard to find the right kind of person because you need to trust them on a deep level. That kind of trust isn't built in a day, but rather it takes a great amount of time before you can consider a person to be a best friend.

Usually friendships of that kind of strength aren't found intentionally, but rather are discovered quite by accident. Either some kind of mutual struggle or need for support brings you closer, or just a long amount of time in which you two have had a relationship.

You don't need a best friend in order to function, but most people would do way better off if they had one.

Community:

The final piece to the belonging puzzle is community. A community is a collection of individuals who are unified for a singular purpose. We can belong to many different types of communities in the world. It used to be that there was very little control over the community that you could be in. In the earlier days of mankind, when you were born in a specific region, you were part of that community, whether you liked it or not. You didn't have much of a choice of whether you participated in the community or not. However, things have since changed due to the fact that we have a greater level of social mobility in the world. We can now choose where we want to live, where we want to work and even which country we are citizens in. This changes the way that we classify community as a whole.

Community is no longer about physical location, but rather it is about ideas. We have the ability to find and form communities based off of interests, concepts and desired outcome. Let's look at what forms a healthy community.

Purpose:

An effective community is unified by a purpose. It can be a major purpose, such as worshipping God at a church, or it can be a fun purpose, such as running a softball league. Every good and healthy community has some kind of purpose that is appealing. The reason behind this is that one of the higher levels of human actualization is the desire to be a part of something bigger than oneself. We as people naturally crave a purpose that goes beyond our own ambitions, primarily because of the fact that we are very aware of our own mortality. Everyone dies and we are actuality aware of this fact. Because we have such a limited time on this earth, it is in the hearts of every person to do something that truly matters.

When there is a presence of a real purpose that adds value to the world and creates meaning in our lives, we respond better. We become more involved in the community, we find ourselves connecting to others on a deeper level. When people are unified for a singular purpose and that purpose is meaningful, the relationships created are stronger and healthier. This is where we get our general sense of belonging from.

Healing:

A community needs to be healing for individuals who are struggling and suffering. What makes a healing community is quite simply an attitude of wanting to care and bring restoration to other members of the community. A good community focuses on creating an atmosphere where an individual knows that he will be well taken care of if he is struggling with something. If he is having health issues, the community moves to help him with practical needs. If he is struggling with emotional problems, the community has people who are willing to listen to him and walk alongside him in his suffering. Most communities lack this healing aspect because they have a strong attitude of saying "it's not my problem." But the issue there is that if you want to have an effective community that is able to empower your members and allow them to achieve greatness in their life, you must be willing to get involved. There is no replacement for a healing community in this world.

Encouragement:

A community also needs to encourage its members continually to strive for the best and most importantly towards the goal. This is where a lot of workplaces fall short. A workplace is a community, but most of the time it is treated as if it were some kind of chore to be there. There is little focus on creating a good community within the workplace because it is seen as cost prohibitive or a waste of time. The truth is that when a workplace becomes a community that is focused on encouragement of the employees, it will increase their productivity, lower their stress and improve their relationship with the company.

The rigors of the workplace are hard. Even when there is monetary compensation, struggles and trials can elicit a great amount of pain and hardship on an employee. Without an environment focused on actively encouraging the employee and pushing them towards greatness, they will eventually fail. A lot of employers believe that just because an employee is doing well currently, that they will always do well. This would be like assuming that just because a car has gasoline in it during a trip, that it will always have gasoline.

Encouragement is the fuel that will allow any employee to continue doing a good job. If they aren't doing well, encouragement will inspire them to move forward. If they are doing well, encouragement will validate them and help them stay the course. Most importantly, encouragement will fuel their natural desire for accomplishment and will help them feel as if they belong within the community.

Ultimately, we can see that there are a great many different aspects of belonging. The thing that ties it all together is our basic human desire to belong to something. We need intimacy, friendship and community if we are going to be able to thrive in the world. If we do not have these three things, it will not allow us to function healthy in the esteem section. How we feel about ourselves greatly relates to how we are connected to the world around us. When we are receiving constant love and joy from the people around us, we experience a great degree of psychological health and freedom. This then allows us to go out into the world and achieve greater things. Most importantly, this effects our own esteem and self-image, which is the next step on the pyramid.

Chapter 5: Esteem Killers

After we have become self-actualized in a group or community setting, we begin to develop a sense of self-consciousness. Without other people, there wouldn't be any reason for us to have a consciousness of self because we would be entirely self-contained. In reality, though, we find that we are connected to the world around us intimately. We become dependent on how people view us and we develop a need for respect, a need to be taken seriously and a need to be held up in high regard. This is what we would refer to as esteem. There is a positive and a negative side of esteem. One of the greatest negatives is the fact that since we do exist in a community, we tend to develop an unhealthy obsession with how people view us.

Esteem is a tricky stage when it comes to self-actualization, primarily due to the fact that in order to have healthy levels of self-esteem, you must be able to simultaneously reject lower levels of thinking and embrace higher levels of your own self-image. There are quite a few barriers that are in the way of developing a healthy level of self-esteem. Let's go ahead and identify all of the barriers before we begin to discuss how to develop healthy esteem.

Barrier One: Dependence

While we are social creatures and a great deal of our self-esteem comes from relationships around us, there is a tremendous danger in becoming dependent upon others for our sense of self-worth. The problem is that when you determine what your self-worth is based on how other people see and treat you, it means that you will be constantly second guessing yourself. People's opinions are constantly shifting and changing, sometimes they are able to have fair evaluations, but for the most part, a person's opinion isn't based entirely on the whole story. This can leave you in a position where you are chasing after their approval in order to feel good about yourself.

Dependence upon other people for a sense of self-worth is akin to chasing the wind. You will never really get what you're looking for. There will be tremendous highs and tremendous lows that come with basing your sense of worth off of other people. When you finally achieve some level of acceptance from others, you will feel amazing, but once you begin to experience rejection or being snubbed, you will feel terrible.

There are many different ways that approval chasing can manifest itself. A person can become a people pleaser, trying to do everything in order to make others happy. The problem is that when you are focusing on making other people happy, you lose sight of your own self and what makes you happy. You'll find yourself stressed out, exhausted and constantly being walked all over. While you might say to yourself, "at least they are happy," the reality is that they are just taking advantage of you. People pleasers only end up making themselves miserable.

Another type of approval chaser is the person who believes that as long as they do nice things, they will be able to earn love. These are the kinds of people who are willing to spend money picking up the bar tab, who will give rides and do other favors for people endlessly. They hope that by doing good things, they will be looked at favorably. But there is a tremendous problem here. The problem is that if your relationship is entirely based off of the good things that you do for someone, it isn't a real friendship but rather it is a transactional relationship. This means that you are essentially trying to buy their love. The danger here is that truthfully you cannot buy a person's love or kindness, but rather you can only cause them to temporarily feel good about you. True love and relationship goes far beyond being willing to do good things for a person, but rather it involves having the willingness to engage in a deeper relationship.

Sometimes it requires conflict and struggle in order for the relationships to grow. Many people can erroneously make the mistake in believing that by avoiding problems, they are creating a healthy relationship but this is actually false. Relationships cannot grow without some kind of struggle. People are different, no two individuals are alike and whenever you have two different people together, there will be conflict. True relationships grow out of healthy conflict, but unhealthy relationships believe that conflict is a bad thing. People who are dependent upon relationships for their own self-worth will often look at conflict as if it were a bad thing, leading them into a place of never truly having the right kind of relationships that will help them grow as people.

Barrier Two: Seeking External Validators

While approval is one powerful type of external validator, there are others. Perhaps one of the most common amongst people who have low levels of self-worth is the idea of fame. To many people, fame is something to crave because it will give them a sense of admiration and acceptance. There are several problems with chasing after fame however. One such problem is that very few people in this world are able to achieve a level of recognition that we would consider to be fame. So, they are stuck chasing after a dream that will realistically only happen to very few people. And since their motivation for fame isn't because they want their art or craft to be recognized, but rather that they want the world to love them, the attempt will probably end up failing miserably.

External validators can feel good in the moment, but ultimately it will just create a desire for more external validation. It is almost like a drug, the better you feel for external reasons, such as fame, wealth, good looks or expensive clothes, the more you will need those external validators. Eventually you will reach a point where you are unable to obtain what you desire or you find that it just doesn't work. This will create a sense of despair and desolation, preventing you from feeling fulfilled. And since you're always searching for the external validation, you'll never quite find true satisfaction. As you will see, real satisfaction of the self must come from within.

Barrier Three: Abuse

Another barrier that can prevent us from developing a health sense of self is previous abuse. The world can be a very cruel place and as we grow up and develop, we are at risk of the cruelty of others. Mean comments, backhanded compliments, nasty words, all of these things can damage a child and that translates directly to a shattered ego. When your sense of self has been damaged by other people, it can be very hard to feel good about yourself. Instead, an inferiority complex can develop and it will actively hamper you from being able to have a healthy life.

The problem with abuse is that it is often deeply rooted and connected to many different events from our lives. Each time we suffer from abuse, it reinforces a specific type of thinking in our brain. When we are told that we are dumb, our brains will eventually come to believe it. These negative beliefs will prevent us from being able to live out happy lives. This poses a unique obstacle when it comes to learning how to develop a sense of self-esteem, primarily because abuse cannot be ignored. It will always contribute to a person's lack of esteem until it is properly handled.

To make the problem worse, when a person is dealing with low self-esteem due to abuse, they might seek out other methods in order to gain their sense of self. They might turn to external validators, or things like drugs and alcohol. They might waste a lot of their life chasing after things to heal them, but only to experience more pain and suffering. Truthfully, there's only one way to experience healing and that is to deal with your abuse and your trauma.

This can be immensely uncomfortable for a myriad of reasons. Perhaps the biggest detractor from dealing with abuse is the fact that when you choose to look directly at it, you will experience pain. That pain can be overwhelming and it can discourage us from wanting to handle the trauma. Yet, unless we are willing to look at it and face our pain, we will never be whole.

Overcoming abuse and trauma is hard. It is not something that you can do overnight and it is certainly not something that should be attempted alone. Rather, you will need guidance from a friend, someone you trust or even a professional therapist. There is nothing wrong with making the decision to get healthier with your life by reaching out to a professional. It will save you a ton of heartache and sorrow in your life. The secret to a healthier and stronger self is to learn how to overcome the abuses and traumas of the past.

All of these barriers can easily detract from your own ability to have high levels of self-esteem. If you want to achieve greatness and self-actualization, then you must be willing to step away from these barriers. It isn't an easy process, of course, because many of our habits and thought processes are geared around finding external validation. The culture that we live in pushes it as if it were the only way to find wholeness. But if you want to be free, you must take a deep breath and make the conscious decision to reject the desire to look outside of yourself for wholeness. Instead, we must focus on achieving a perfect sense of self-esteem by looking inward for satisfaction and validation.

Chapter 6: True Self-Esteem

If we are going to be truly free and self-actualized individuals, we must have a high degree of esteem. We must be able to feel comfortable in our own skin, regardless of the situation. We must feel strong and confident, we must be able to walk into a room without worrying about what others are thinking about us. Yet, reaching this place isn't particularly easy. It requires a conscious effort on our part if we are going to be able to hold ourselves in high regard.

The higher levels of self-esteem are divided into three areas: competence, self-reliance, and confidence. Once you have mastery over these three areas, you will find that your self-esteem will be relatively high. The most important thing to note about all three of these areas is that they come entirely from within. All of these are driven by determination and a conscious effort on your part. You cannot purchase these things from a store nor can other people add them into you. You must cultivate and develop them on your own.

      Think of your self-esteem like a flower. It can exist in various different stages, it can be tall and healthy, with bright petals and green leaves, or it can be withered and weak. Either way, it is your responsibility with how you are going to take care of the flower. You can find ways to help the flower grow, or you can choose to allow it to stay in whatever state it currently is in. Many people who have low levels of self-esteem make the assumption that they cannot change. The truth is, a self-actualized person has the capacity and ability to choose if they want to change their own esteem levels. As long as you decide that you want to, you can change too! All you have to do is commit to cultivating your esteem and focusing on developing the three attributes below.

Competence:

The first part of gaining a strong level of self-esteem is having the ability to know that you are fairly competent in life. Competency goes beyond skill, rather it is about having the ability to handle problems and struggles in life without being overwhelmed by them. There are a few things to make up competency as a whole.

Competence One Experience:

In order to feel competent at whatever task if before us, we must have sufficient experience with hardship and struggle. A lot of people tend to shy away from new experiences because they feel uncomfortable dealing with the struggle and hardship of trying something new. Instead, they'd prefer to stay in their comfort zone and never overcome their initial fears. This prevents them from having experience and ultimately prevents them from becoming competent.

When it comes to competency, there are universal truths across the board. Experience is the first universal truth. You won't be good at anything without the proper amount of experience practicing, trying and making mistakes. It doesn't matter what the subject matter is, if you want to become a competent individual, you must embrace the fact that you need to spend time to achieve mastery. People who are looking for instant mastery or some kind of bypass to avoid working for their skills will quickly fizzle out. Everyone knows that one guy who is always trying to get ahead, but won't put in the time necessary. No one would consider that individual to be very competent, would they?

Experience is the gatekeeper to competency. If you want to become a competent individual, then you must be willing to do it right by spending time on whatever subject it is. As long as you have a willingness to put in the effort and learn, you will be competent in whatever field you are working in.

Competence Two Self-Education:

Another piece to growing competent is having the ability to learn on your own. We live in a world where there is tremendous amount of information available at our fingertips. The schooling systems we've grown up in really stressed dependence on learning material ahead of time in preparation of taking a test. However, this system creates a form of dependence on being spoon fed information. We are taught that information comes to us, we aren't required to seek it out. Unfortunately, this style of learning is immensely out of date, because we have the power to learn just about anything at any time. Our phones contain the secrets of the universe, all we have to do is look for them.

If you want to be competent across the board, then you must have an attitude of self-education. You must be willing to take it upon yourself to learn everything about a subject that you are wanting mastery over. We live in a world where you can easily access Youtube videos, take online classes and access dozens of self-help websites at a click of a button. Truthfully, no matter what the subject is, there is no excuse for not having sufficient knowledge of a subject matter.

Self-Reliance:

One theme that we have had throughout this book is the theme of being willing to be reliant on your own self. Self-actualization requires that you have a high degree of independence. This doesn't mean that you can't rely on other people, but rather it means that you look to yourself for survival. When you feel like you can trust yourself, when you know that you have the capability to take care of yourself, you will feel supremely confident. Your self-esteem will increase based on how well you trust yourself.

There are a few philosophies that go into self-reliance. Let's look at each part.

Self-Reliance Philosophy One: Reject Entitlement

The first step to accepting a philosophy of self-reliance is to realize that no one in this world is going to do anything for you. It is very easy to be entitled in this current generation, there are a lot of people who believe that they are owed something by the world. They go around expecting people to help them achieve their hopes and dreams. They think that just because they want something, they are entitled to get it. They don't believe in the principles of hard work in order to achieve their goals.

Entitlement is one of the greatest killers of self-esteem. When you are entitled, you come under the idea that other people are responsible for your success. An entitled mindset doesn't focus on relying on the self, but rather focuses on other people's actions.

Signs of an entitled mindset include:

- Inability to accept responsibility for one's own actions
- Blaming others for your failures
- Making excuses that are based on external factors
- Expecting other people to help you for free

All of these things will contribute to a tremendous level of entitlement. The opposite of entitlement would be merit. It is the idea that rather than being *owed* something, that you must instead choose to *earn* it. By focusing on earning instead of being owed, you will be required to work for the things that you want. This breeds a strong level of self-reliance because you are focusing on achieving things by yourself, instead of hoping other people will make beneficial decisions for you.

Self-Reliant Philosophy Two: Embrace Hardship

The self-reliant individual is the one who is able to endure a great deal of trials and struggles in order to achieve their objectives. Struggle and trials bring discomfort, however, and discomfort can greatly discourage a person from wanting to rely solely on their own selves. If you are afraid of conflict and struggle, then you will never be able to rely on yourself in a serious crisis. Fear and frustration can push you backwards and cripple your ability to make decisions. When things get really tough, a self-reliant person doesn't freeze up, but rather is capable of dealing with the trouble. Someone who is dependent upon others will end up losing control and look to someone else to help them. The problem is that if there isn't someone else around, they are essentially in trouble. They will not have the ability to handle their crisis well.

Hardship is a fact of life. We will endure pain and misery in our lives, there is no getting around that. If you want to become more reliant on yourself, you must come to realize that pain and suffering are a guarantee and you must be prepared for it all times. Not only that, but you must be willing to embrace hardship. Self-reliance requires resilience. It requires the ability to endure suffering so that you can thrive in it. When a person endures suffering without resilience, the suffering and struggle usually breaks them. It affects them negatively and prevents them from being able to grow.

Yet, when there is struggle, there is an opportunity to grow from it. The Stoics from Ancient Greece and Roman times believed that preparing and expecting hardship would lead to the ability to overcome emotional struggle. Rather than shy away from danger, they would prepare for it and embrace it. This would lead to a diminished effect that hardship would have on one's emotions and feelings, allowing one to overcome all challenges.

Confidence:

When you combine competency and self-reliance, you find that you have a higher degree of confidence in your own self. The word confidence means having the ability to trust in something, knowing that it will stand firm. When you have confidence in yourself, it means that you are able to trust yourself in just about any situation. A lot of times confidence gets confused with swagger. Just because someone is loud, braggadocios and seems not to care about what other people say, it doesn't mean that he is confident. It means that he is acting confident.

Confidence is a much deeper matter than how you act on the inside, rather it is about how you feel internally when you are confronting things that make you uncomfortable. Regardless of whether you are asking someone out on a date, trying to get a raise or just simply entering a room, confidence is necessary for you to feel at ease and normal. *Feelings* are a lot different than actions, however. Someone can act very confident, but is actually feeling nervous the entire time.

A self-actualized individual finds confidence deep from within, knowing that they can trust themselves in just about any situation. This allows them to feel safe and secure, insulating them from the negative emotions that are present when you aren't confidence. Let's look at some habits that will help cultivate a stronger sense of self-confidence.

Confidence Habit One: Positive Self Talk

We all speak to ourselves mentally. There is a voice in our heads that either can be a very powerful motivation tool, or it can be extremely negative for us. We develop this self-talking voice from a very early age and it is influenced by our thoughts. The more negative thoughts that we have, the more negative that our self-talk will become. Negative self-talk can quickly rob us of our confidence, telling us that we cannot achieve great things or that we are worthless.

The easiest solution to dealing with negative self-talk is to learn how to have positive self-talking techniques. It is just a practice of saying "I can" mentally instead of saying "I can't." Over time, you will find that the more positive self-talk you engage in, the more confident you will become in your own self.

Confidence Habit Two: Be prepared

Our emotional state going into uncertain situations can often be quite low. We can feel frantic or nervous, but these feelings of fear come from dealing with the unknown. It is far better to be prepared, because preparation gives you glimpses of the unknown. You won't have to be nervous if you know the subject matter well, whatever it is. Preparation is a habit, however. If you make a habit of focusing on always being prepared, you will feel significantly more confident with your life.

Confidence Habit Three: Stance

Believe it or not, but there is one simple trick that you can do to improve your sense of confidence. That trick is stance. Science has proven, that if you are willing to stand up straight and puff out your chest, you will begin to feel more confident. A slumped over body position and a hunched back can easily lead a person to feel as if they are smaller than they actually are. If you want to feel more confident, you must adopt power stances that keep your body upright. After a while, you will begin to feel more comfortable standing that way.

When you combine all of these attributes together, you will find that you are going to have a higher level of natural self-esteem. The best part about this is the fact that it all comes from within. You do not need someone else to help you achieve these, but rather you can cultivate these habits and philosophies that you can become self-actualized.

Chapter 7: Are You Actualized?

The final piece of the pyramid is nothing more than a culmination of all of the other blocks that have been built. Once you have mastered all four areas, you will naturally become self-actualized. This will allow for you to live a fundamentally happier and more fulfilling life. You will be able to become an exceptional individual and achieve anything that you put your mind to!

So, you must be able to properly evaluate where you are on this pyramid if you are going to begin to change. Below is a questionnaire for you to be able to identify where your strengths and weaknesses are when it comes to self-actualization. You can see how many of your needs are being fulfilled based off of each question. Each time you answer yes, that counts as one need being fulfilled, but each time you answer no, it is an indicator of a lack of a need.

Tally up the score for each section and see how well you are doing with every area.

Physical Needs:

I am acutely aware of my health needs and take care of them.

I know what my nutritional intake is on a daily basis.

I am physically fit enough to run a mile

I do not worry about lifting heavy things

Safety:

I do not have to worry about my safety.

I can handle myself in a fight.

I have a steady grasp on my finances

I have a budget

My relationships treat me well

Love and Belonging:

I feel loved

I have a close, intimate relationship

I have a best friend

I'm in a community that takes care of me

I feel connected to my relationships

I like my community

Self-Esteem

I feel good about myself

I'm not worried about how other people see me

I don't need other people's respect

I'm able to be alone and still happy.

I am confident

I am able to get things done without others helping me

I know I can survive in a serious crisis

Score:

22: Perfection! You are self-actualized!

19-21: You are definitely a higher functioning individual

15-18: You are a very capable individual

10-14: There is lots of room for you to grow

5-9: You have a lot of unmet needs

0-5: Your needs are seriously neglected

So how did you do on the test? Did you score high or low? Either way, don't allow these numbers to create a sensation of shame within you. A low score is nothing more than an indicator how far you have to go. It gives you a better sense of where you actually are at. When we have unmet needs, we begin to suffer from a great deal of imbalances and emotional struggles. Having a clear idea of which needs are unmet will give you the ability to actually correct those needs. Look at each area that you answered no and ask yourself, how can I fix this? You have the power to make serious changes in your life. It won't be easy and it won't necessarily be fun, but it is possible.

Self-actualization is all about accepting your own responsibility to yourself. Maslow once said, "What a man can be, he must be." This quote means that if you have the capacity to become an exceptional person, then it is your moral duty and obligation. That means that you must focus on becoming the best person that you can be.

We make a lot of mistakes when we come to believe that only special people are capable of achieving extraordinary things. We might even be convinced that we can never be extraordinary ourselves. The truth is that everyone is born with the same capacity for greatness, but different people have different motivators. A self-actualized person is motivated by one and only one thing: himself. He is able to achieve amazing things because there is a strong drive within him to excel. This drive comes from the desire to be the best he can be. It is not driven by other needs, because those needs are already fulfilled. The secret to becoming driven by yourself is to secure all of your other needs, leaving you free to focus on excellence without stress or worry. Having all of your needs met ultimately leads to the greatest freedom that a person can experience.

Conclusion

As we can see, human beings are incredibly complicated creatures. We might think that needs are simple at the beginning. We might think all that a child needs to survive is food and shelter, but as we have seen here, there is far more involved with meeting needs. Each level of the pyramid is closely connected to one another and whenever we attain mastery over one, we find that we get closer to self-actualization. Once we reach the highest level, we are finally free and capable of doing whatever we wish to do. The freedom from bondage is worth the price of admission.

The road to self-actualization isn't an easy one. Our modern-day culture creates a lot of roadblocks that prevent us from being able to focus on the deeper levels of community, relationship and introspection. Jealousy, fear, negativity, all of these things work together to prevent us from being able to get our needs met through legitimate means. Instead, we find ourselves living in a world that is obsessed with finding fulfillment in things that are only meant to enhance life. There are a great many things like validation, pleasure, fun, alcohol, sports, video games that can enhance our lives, but none of those things give our lives meaning. No needs can be met through pleasure, nor validation. Imagine these things as if they were sprinkles atop a cake. There is nothing wrong with sprinkles, but you would be hard pressed to find a person who would prefer to eat a bowl of sprinkles as opposed to a cake. Yet we live in a world of people filling their bowls with only sprinkles and trying desperately to convince themselves that they are eating cake.

Don't be like those who are chasing after the wind in vain. The greatest pleasure, the greatest source of validation, is being your own ruler. There is nothing better than being the captain of your own destiny. There is satisfaction in being able to drive your ship to wherever you want to go. It isn't easy, at times it will be rather difficult and you might feel a desire to quit. But the road to self-actualization requires you to push yourself past the comfortable parts of your life in order to achieve greatness. Those who are self-actualized run this world, do you want to be one of them?

Other books available by Landon T. Smith on Kindle, paperback and audio:

Why NLP Isn't Working For You

The Art of Influence

The Power of Reflection: Embrace Your Past to Find a Purpose for Your Future

Card Declined: Learn to Set Priorities So You Stop Overspending

Made in the USA
San Bernardino, CA
03 January 2018